John
To:

Angela
From:

Sales Motivation

Great Quotes to Fire Your Passion

Todd Duncan

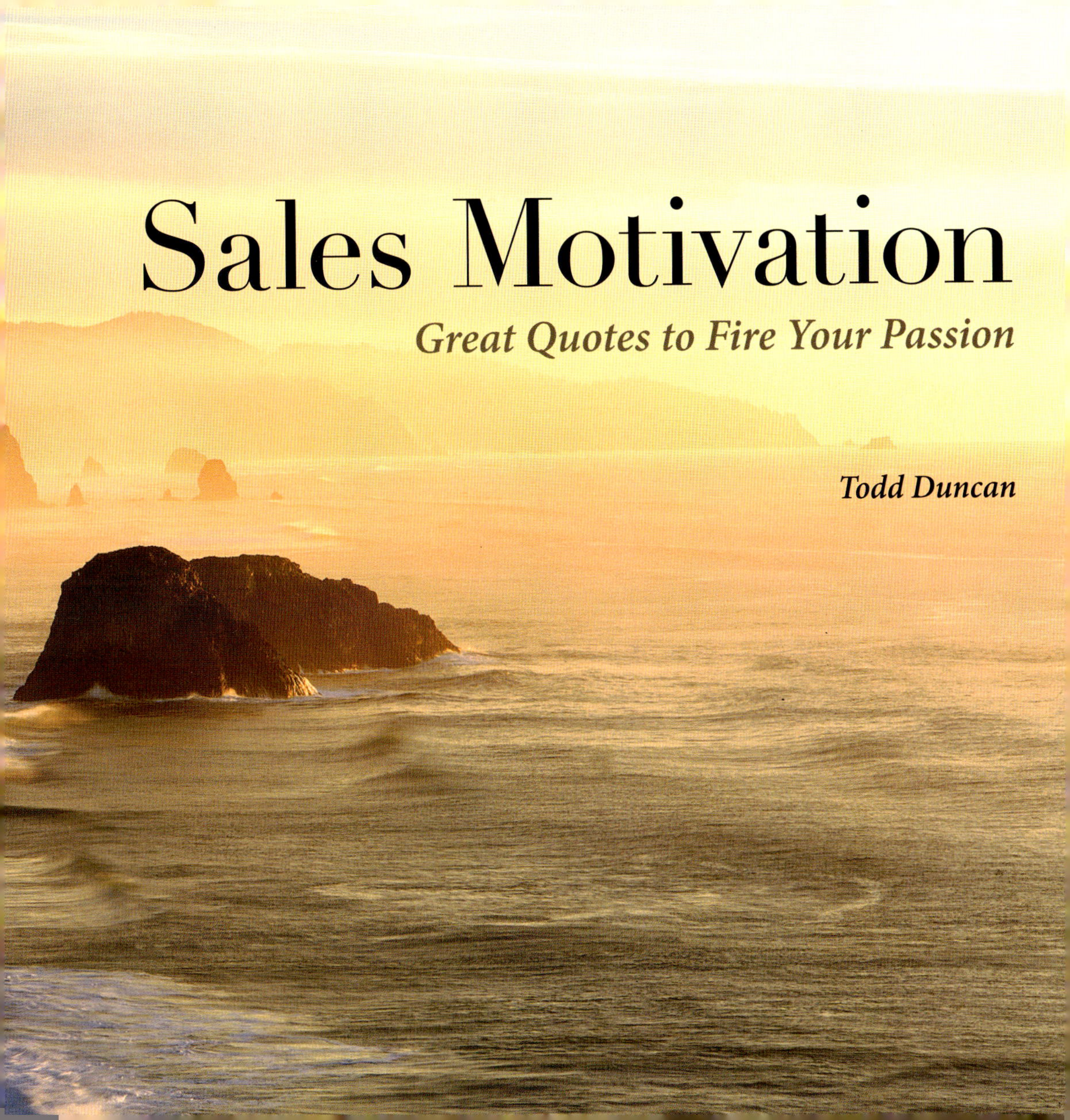

Design: Vieceli Design Company, West Dundee, Illinois
Editing: Jennifer Svoboda

My thanks to some of the great photographers whose photos are featured in this book.

Todd and Brad Reed *(www.toddreedphoto.com; phone 231-843-0777)*
Photos by Todd Reed on pages: front endleaf, 2, 10-11, 13, 20-21, 28-29, 34-35, 39, 40-41, 55, 59, 62-63, 82-83, 85, 92, 93, 98-99

Photos by Brad Reed on pages: 14-15, 69, 89, 105

Ken Jenkins *(www.kenjenkins.com)*
Photos on pages: cover, 8, 18, 27, 44-45, 66, 80-81, 90-91, 102-103, 112

Steve Terrill *(www.steveterrill.com)*
Photos on pages: 1, 23, 30-31, 36, 48-49, 52-53, 66-67, 72, 74-75, 76-77, 114

Bruce Heinemann *(www.theartofnature.com)*
Photos on pages: back cover, 50, 52-53, 97

Tom Henry *Photos on pages: 16-17*

Published by Simple Truths, an imprint of Sourcebooks, Inc.
P.O. Box 4410, Naperville, Illinois 60567-4410
(630) 961-3900
Fax: (630) 961-2168

Table of Contents

• Introduction •

Success is a daily decision!

Show me a successful person and I will show you someone who chooses the course of success over and over in their life. I will show you a person who is full of passion, excitement, courage, conviction, focus, positivity and enthusiasm. Successful people who exude these attributes attract all kinds of positive results into their life; more business, deeper relationships, improved health and overall happiness. They are the winners who can get up when the odds are against them, when the circumstances look the worst, and when it would be easy to give up.

Ever since I was a young boy, I have chosen this course of success, and quotes fired my passion. My first memorized quote was from Napolean Hill; "Whatever the mind can conceive and believe it can achieve." It was this quote that ignited my passion to live a life of affirmation and what inspired me to write this book, Sales Motivation. I love quotes, and they are a part of my daily vitamins – they are to my soul and heart and mind what normal vitamins are to my health, body and stamina.

A daily dose of positivity from some of the most respected thought leaders ever might be all you need to succeed, sell more, make more, and enjoy life to the fullest.

Here's to you taking a "quote today".

action

Every morning in Africa, a gazelle wakes up. It knows it must run faster than the fastest lion or it will be killed...every morning a lion wakes up. It knows it must outrun the slowest gazelle or it will starve to death. It doesn't matter whether you're a lion or a gazelle...when the sun comes up, you'd better be running.

— Anonymous

ACTION CONQUERS
FEAR.
— PETER ZARLENGA

In any moment of decision, the BEST THING you can do is the RIGHT THING; the next best thing is the WRONG THING; and the worst thing you can do is NOTHING.

— Theodore Roosevelt

attitude

A positive attitude is a powerful force.

— Anonymous

It's our attitude
in life that
determines life's
attitude towards us.

— Earl Nightingale

CHANGE YOUR THOUGHTS AND CHANGE YOUR WORLD.

— NORMAN VINCENT PEALE

The longer I live, the more I realize the impact of attitude on life. Attitude, to me, is more important than the facts.

It is more important than the past, than education, than money, than circumstances, than failures, than successes, than what other people think or say or do. It is more important than appearance, giftedness, or skill. It will make or break a company… a church… a home.

The remarkable thing is we have a choice every day regarding the attitude we will embrace for that day. We cannot change our pasts, we cannot change the fact that people will act in a certain way. We cannot change the inevitable. The only thing we can do is play on the one string we have, and that is our attitude.

I am convinced that life is 10 percent what happens and 90 percent how I react to it. And so it is with you — we are in charge of our attitudes.

— Charles Swindoll

Think big thoughts, but relish small pleasures.
— H. Jackson Brown

balance

In the time of your life, LIVE.

— Anonymous

Things that matter most must never be at the mercy of things that matter least.

— Van Goethe

The only thing that stands between a person and what they want from life is often the will to try it and the faith to believe it's possible.

— Rich Devos

belief

EFFORT ONLY FULLY RELEASES ITS REWARD AFTER A PERSON REFUSES TO QUIT.

— Napoleon Hill

Belief fuels passion, and…passion rarely fails.

— M. Anderson

challenges

In the middle of every difficulty comes opportunity.

— Albert Einstein

Kites rise highest against the wind… not with it.

— Winston Churchill

ADVERSITY is the first path to truth.
— George Gordon Byron

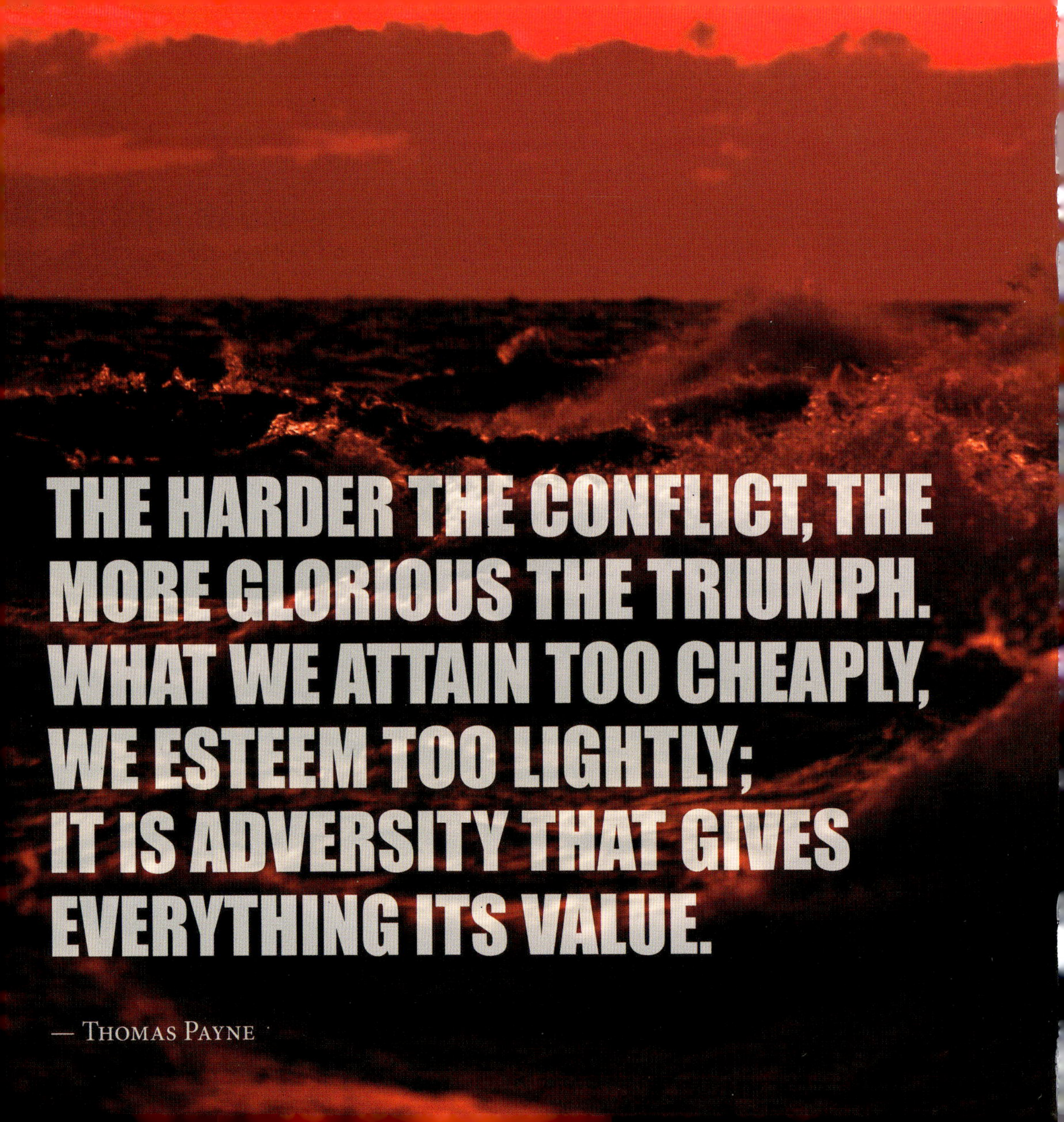
THE HARDER THE CONFLICT, THE MORE GLORIOUS THE TRIUMPH. WHAT WE ATTAIN TOO CHEAPLY, WE ESTEEM TOO LIGHTLY; IT IS ADVERSITY THAT GIVES EVERYTHING ITS VALUE.
— Thomas Payne

commitment

The man on top of the mountain didn't fall there.

— Anonymous

The *difference* between
and others is not a
a *lack of knowledge,*
lack of will.

a successful person
lack of strength, not
but rather a

— Vince Lombardi

courage

Fear is a reaction. Courage is a decision.

— Winston Churchill

ALL OF YOUR DREAMS CAN COME TRUE IF YOU HAVE THE COURAGE TO PURSUE THEM.

— WALT DISNEY

Courage is the door that can only be opened from the inside.

— Terry Neil

It is not the critic who counts: not the man who points out how the strong man stumbles or where the doer of deeds could have done better. The credit belongs to the man who is actually in the arena, whose face is marred by dust and sweat and blood, who strives valiantly; who errs and comes up short again and again, because there is no effort without error or shortcoming, but who knows the great enthusiasms, the great devotions, who spends himself for a worthy cause; who, at the best, knows, in the end, the triumph of high achievement, and who, at the worst, if he fails, at least he fails while daring greatly, so that his place shall never be with those cold and timid souls who know neither victory nor defeat.

— Theodore Roosevelt

Courage is resistance to fear,
the mastery of fear...
not the absence of fear.

— Mark Twain

creativity

The world is but a canvas to the imagination.

— Henry David Thoreau

THE ENTREPRENEUR

They cast aside their assurance for a 40-hour week; they leave the safe cover of tenure and security...and charge across the perilous fields of change and opportunity. If they succeed, their profits will not come from what they take from their fellow citizens, but from the value they freely place on the gift of their imagination.

— George Gilder

desire

The longer I live, the more I am certain that the difference between great and weak men is simply an invincible determination.

— Sir Thomas Buxton

PEOPLE ARE
LIKE STICKS OF
DYNAMITE...

THE POWER'S ON THE INSIDE
BUT NOTHING HAPPENS
UNTIL THE FUSE GETS LIT.

— M. Anderson

It is easier to go down the mountain than up,

but the view from the top is the best.

— Anonymous

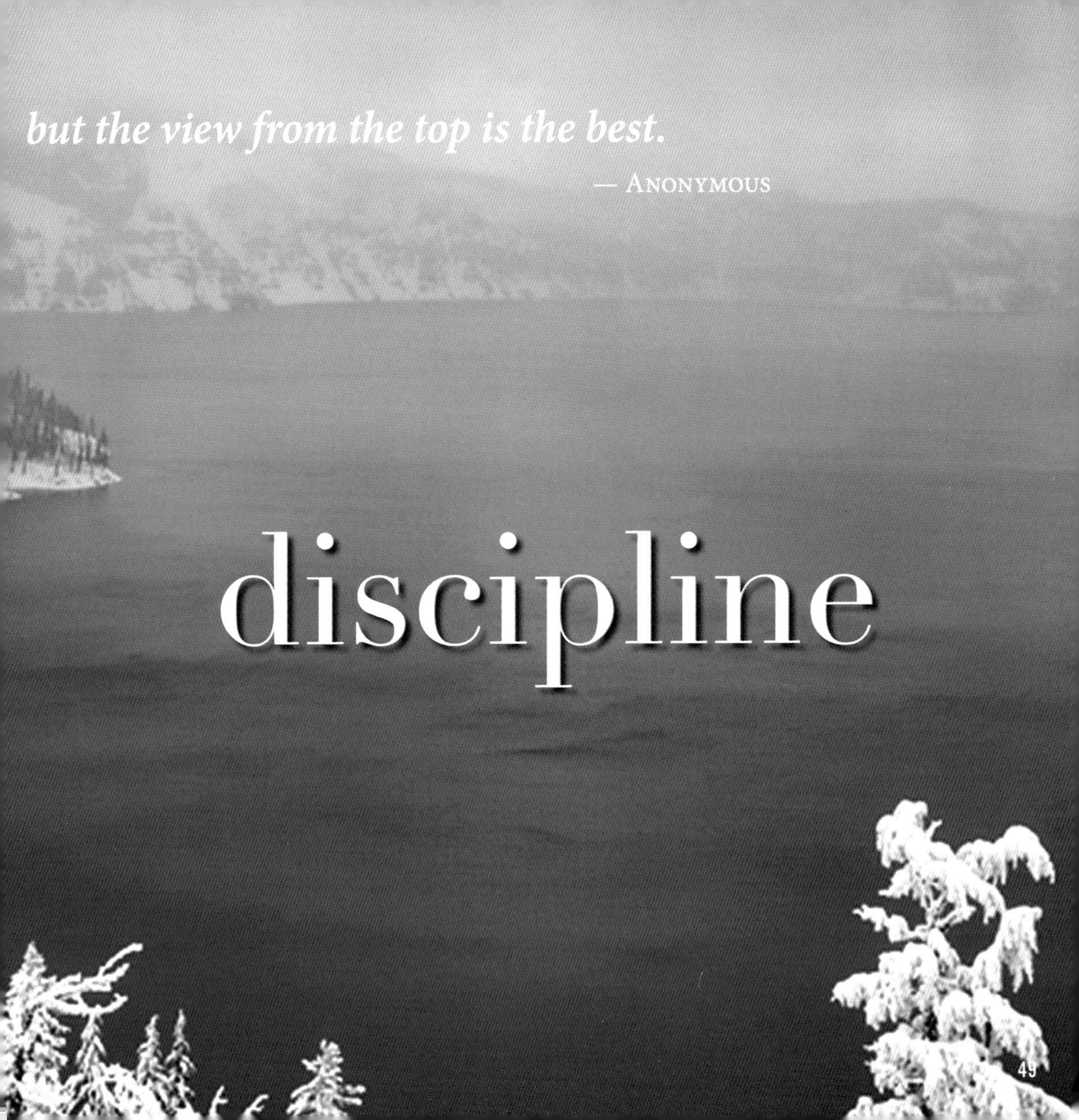

discipline

Self-respect is the fruit of discipline.
— Abraham J. Heschel

To get what we've never had, we must do what we've never done.

— Anonymous

Far away there in the sunshine
are my highest aspirations.
I may not reach them,
but I can look up and see their beauty,
believe in them, and try to
follow where they lead.
— Louisa May Alcott

dreams

If one advances confidently in the direction of their dreams and endeavors to live the life they've imagined, they will meet success unexpected in common hours.

— David Thoreau

Nothing happens but first a dream. — Carl Sandburg

excellence

The difference in success or failure can be doing something nearly right...or doing it exactly right.

— Anonymous

Quality is never an accident; it is always the result of high intention, sincere effort and skillful execution. It represents the *wise choice* of many alternatives.

— Will A. Foster

It is a funny thing about life:
if you refuse to accept anything but the best,
you very often get it.

— Somerset Maugham

The *quality* of a person's
proportion to
excellence, regardless
field of endeavor.

life is in direct
their *commitment* to
of their chosen

— Vince Lombardi

failure

Failure is an opportunity to begin again more intelligently.
— Henry Ford

When it is dark enough, you can see the stars.
— Ralph Waldo Emerson

FAILURES ARE DIVIDED INTO TWO CLASSES — THOSE WHO THOUGHT AND NEVER DID AND THOSE WHO DID AND NEVER THOUGHT.

— John Charles Sak

Focus on the critical few, not the insignificant many.

— Anonymous

focus

If you chase two rabbits
both will escape.

— Chinese Proverb

Learn to set your course by the stars, not by the lights of every passing ship.

— General Omar Bradley

goals

The most important thing about goals is…
having one.

— Geoffry Abert

Goals are dreams
with deadlines.

— Diana S. Hunt

The world has a habit of making room for the person whose words and actions show that they know where they're going.

— Napoleon Hill

growth

Unless you try to do something beyond what you

have already mastered, you will never grow.

— Ronald E. Osborn

THE GEM CANNOT BE POLISHED WITHOUT
FRICTION,

NOR THE MAN PERFECTED WITHOUT TRIALS.

— Chinese Proverb

We are what we repeatedly do.
Excellence, then, is not an act, but a habit.
— Aristotle
habits

WE FIRST MAKE OUR HABITS,

AND THEN THEY MAKE US.

— John Dryden

integrity

Wisdom is knowing the right path to take… integrity is taking it.

— M. H. McKee

THE LONGER
WE FOLLOW
THE RIGHT PATH,
THE EASIER
IT BECOMES.

— English Proverb

A QUIET CONSCIENCE SLEEPS IN THUNDER.

— English Proverb

knowledge

Knowledge is like climbing a mountain; the higher you reach, the more you can see and appreciate. — Anonymous

Chance favors the prepared mind.

— Louis Pasteur

Learn as if you were going to live forever, live as if you were going to die tomorrow.
— Mahatma Gandhi

passion

Nothing great was ever accomplished without enthusiasm.

— Ralph Waldo Emerson

Many things will catch your eye, but only a few will catch your heart...PURSUE THOSE.
— Anonymous

The best way to succeed is to discover what you love and find a way to offer it to others.

— Oprah Winfrey

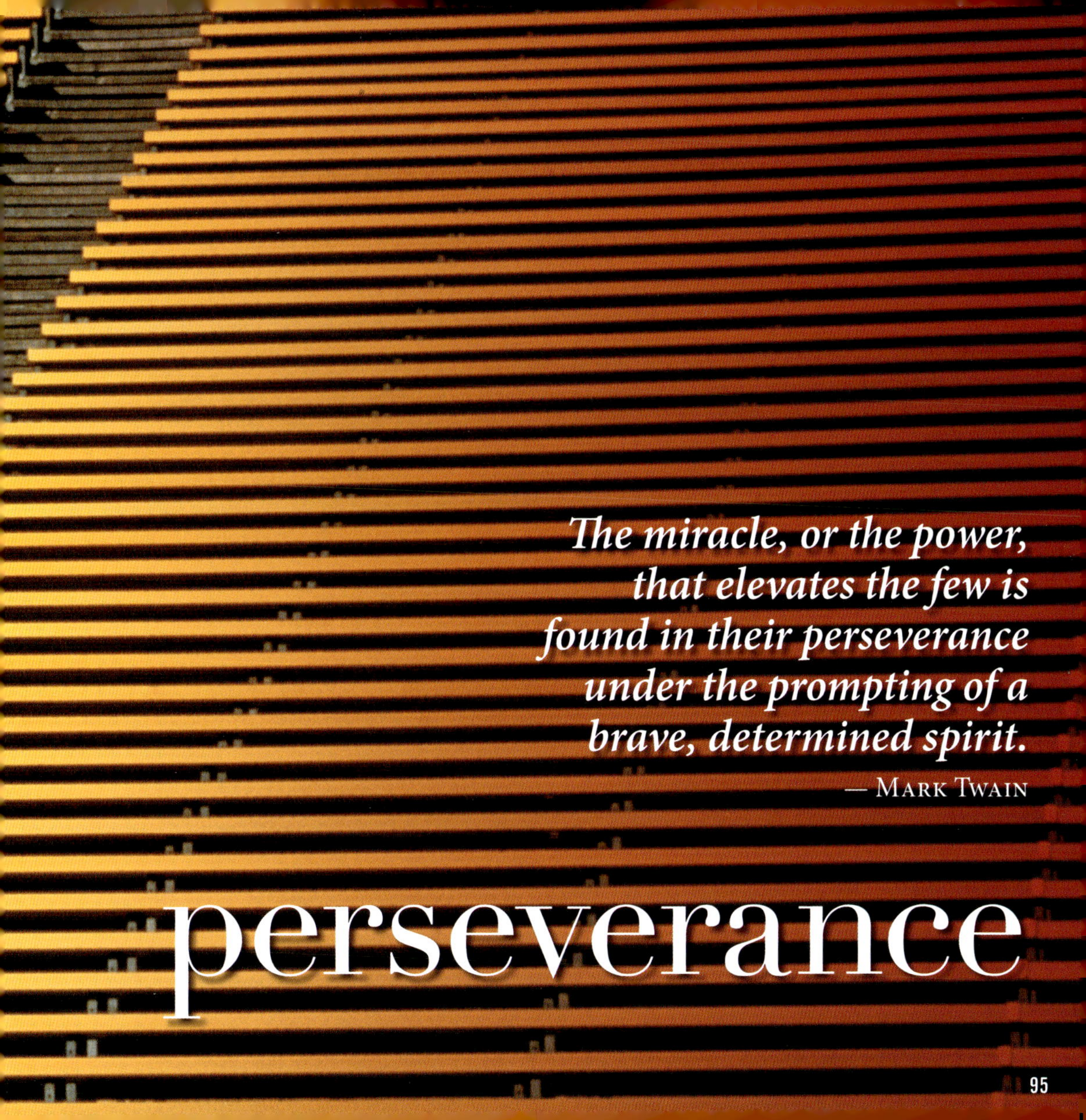

The miracle, or the power, that elevates the few is found in their perseverance under the prompting of a brave, determined spirit.

— Mark Twain

perseverance

Nothing in the world can take the place of persistence. Talent will not; nothing is more common that unsuccessful men with talent. Genius will not; unrewarded genius is almost a proverb. Education will not; the world is full of educated derelicts. **Persistence and determination alone are omnipotent.**

— Calvin Coolidge

In the confrontation between
the stream and the rock,
the stream always wins…
not through strength but
by perseverance.

— H. Jackson Brown

I am the master of my fate;
I am the captain of my soul.

— William E. Henley

responsibility

Win without boasting. Lose without excuses.

— Vince Lombardi

EXCUSES
ARE THE NAILS USED
TO BUILD A HOUSE
OF FAILURE.

— Don Wilder

risk

Don't be afraid to take a big step if needed.
You can't cross a chasm in two small jumps.

— Anonymous

YOU WILL ALWAYS MISS 100% OF THE SHOTS YOU DON'T TAKE.

— *Wayne Gretzky*

You cannot discover new oceans unless you have the courage to lose sight of the shore.

— Anonymous

service

It is one of the greatest compensations in life that no one can help another without helping themselves.

— Ralph Waldo Emerson

Life is like a game of tennis; the player who serves well seldom loses.

— Anonymous

Customer service *is not* a department…
it's an attitude.

— M. Anderson

Our *purpose* is not to complain about the steepness of the climb, but *to help each other* on the way that is *often difficult* and *sometimes perilous*. And in the end, all that we do should not be done to glorify ourselves, but *to serve others*.

— Oliver North

success

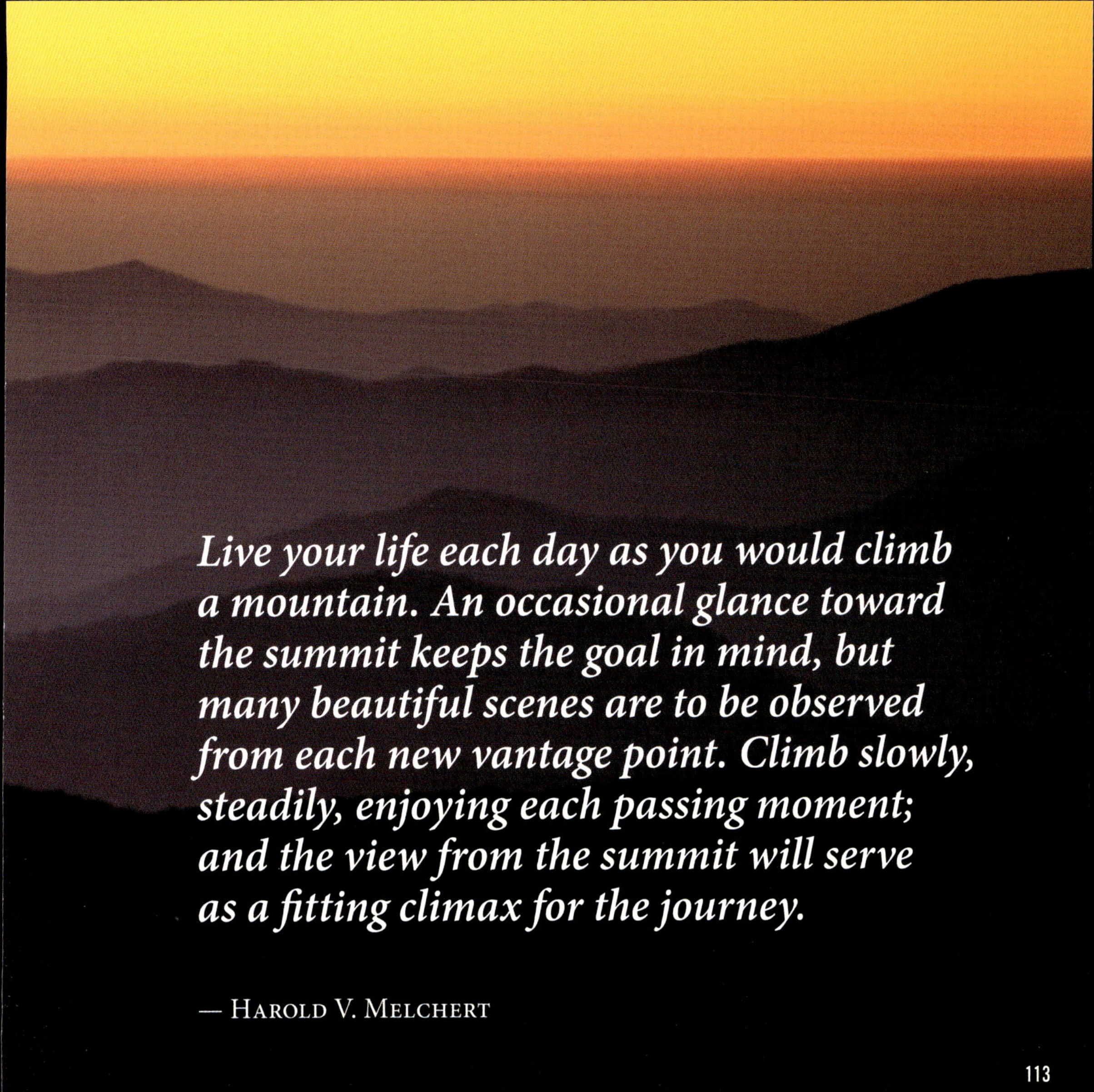

Live your life each day as you would climb a mountain. An occasional glance toward the summit keeps the goal in mind, but many beautiful scenes are to be observed from each new vantage point. Climb slowly, steadily, enjoying each passing moment; and the view from the summit will serve as a fitting climax for the journey.

— Harold V. Melchert

Success is a *journey*, not a *destination*.

— Anonymous

It is not the things we get, but the hearts we touch, that will measure our success in life.

— Anonymous

IF A PERSON
THEIR BEST,
IS THERE?

HAS DONE WHAT ELSE

— George S. Patton

• Todd Duncan •

Extensive biography

For over two decades, Todd Duncan has been a friend and mentor to millions of ambitious professionals worldwide. Since the age of twenty-three he has lived in the trenches and knows what it takes to succeed amidst the rising pressures and incessant temptations of the marketplace. It is from this platform that he teaches and touches the lives of some 300,000 professionals every year.

Inc., CNN Money, SUCCESS, Fox Business, Investor's Business Daily, Entrepreneur, and *Washington Business Journal* are just a short sampling of the numerous media outlets who have featured Duncan's material. As an author, his books have landed on prestigious bestseller lists including the *New York Times, Los Angeles Times, Wall Street Journal, Barnes & Noble, Amazon.com, CEOread.com,* and *BusinessWeek* and are now in 30 languages world-wide.

TODD'S JOURNEY

Todd has always been highly motivated but his ambition didn't at first lead to true success. By the age of 27, he was listed in the top one-percent of his industry, earning hundreds of thousands a year but his world was dangerously out of balance. Eventually, his personal empire of expensive toys and fast living was toppled by a two-year cocaine addiction. On his way down, he faced up to his shortcomings and thus embarked on a road to recovery and redemption.

Through the support of friends and mentors like John Maxwell, Zig Ziglar, Og Mandino and Ken Blanchard, Todd not only recovered but quickly re-ascended to the top. At thirty he founded his first training company and began researching successful people in all walks of business and life. Over the past two decades, Todd has built a respected worldwide enterprise while continuing to observe and study the lives of achievers who thrive on and off the job. His ongoing discoveries are synthesized into compelling resources for living in a meaningful, enriching and profitable way. His best-selling books and popular seminars have influenced millions to pursue a generous and abundant life.

TODD'S CONTENT

Todd's blockbuster title, *High Trust Selling*, has revolutionized the mindset of the sales industry. Resulting from over twenty years of market research and analysis, the book unpacks proven principles by which salespeople can establish long-lasting and high-yielding bonds of trust with their clients. In *High Trust Selling*, Todd distills these principles into fourteen clear-cut laws. The book has been lauded as required reading for professionals around the globe and has become a cornerstone resource of numerous corporations.

Todd's next blockbuster, *Time Traps*, made the *New York Times* bestseller six weeks after its release. In it, Duncan offers proven remedies for being swamped and reveals how to set a schedule that works every day. The principles in *Time Traps* have been hailed as a revolutionary that finally teaches professionals how to boost their careers while decreasing their work hours and make more money in the process.

TODD'S COMPANY

In 1992, Todd founded The Duncan Group to meet the growing demand for innovative training and leadership in the mortgage banking industry where he began his career. In subsequent years, The Duncan Group has expanded its scope of operations to influence the general market and has earned its reputation as one of the elite personal development companies in the world.

Captivating as a speaker and author and admired as a leader, Todd Duncan's passion is to unlock the potential in every individual crossing his path. In designing world-renowned content and universal success strategies, Todd's ultimate goal is to help people lead healthy lives of fulfillment and satisfaction.

Todd and his two sons and live in Newport Beach, California.

You can contact Todd Duncan at:

Todd Duncan
The Duncan Group
(858) 551-0920 Office
www.toddduncan.com